OUTRAGEOUS *Ads*

RED ROCK PRESS

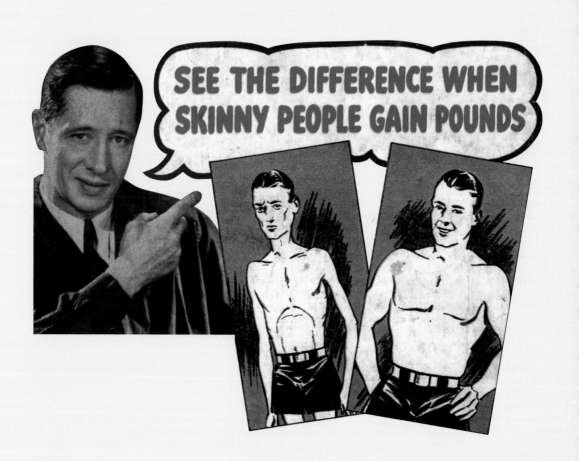

Contents

Introduction

So what *does* the doctor smoke? Pretty much anything, if you believe the ads in this book! Yes, when these doctors aren't busy telling us to drink whisky and eat sweets, they're falling over themselves to endorse their favorite cigarettes. Sometimes elbowing sports stars out of the way to do so.

It's not just the way the medical and sport professions were used to sell unsuitable products that seems strange to modern sensibilities – can you imagine a modern weight-loss advertisement headed "Fat Folk"?

And if you think the means of selling is odd—look at the products themselves! They range from a belt that electrocutes its wearer to provide "vigour" to a "Chin Reducer and Beautifier" contraption that looks more like a torture device.

Funny and ridiculous as they undoubtedly are, deliberate humor doesn't play a big part in these ads, maybe because it's only in retrospect that we can see that

Dri-Poo for the hair might not be the most savory of names, or that a horse

exercise machine (guaranteed satisfaction) might find its real market in sexually-

frustrated Victorian housewives.

But perhaps the real reason the ads in this book make us laugh out loud is because they come from eras with completely different ideas and values from ours— where pesticide-covered oranges were a good thing and sunlamps were genuinely

used to ward off the flu in children.

And that's the warning these ads should give us. We may think we're more

sophisticated now, but under all the gloss of modern marketing, has much really

changed? Next time you're convinced you need the latest must-have product,

look back at this book and beware!

Drink for health

Alcohol has always been used for medicinal purposes, but you don't get many ads nowadays that sell it as a curative first and foremost, before the fun and relaxation element, or the "get out of your tree and forget the mess you've made of your miserable life" one. Still, it's a lot easier to justify buying whiskey by the caseload if it's your medicine cabinet you're restocking instead of the bar. Not that the people in these ads are a great recommendation for the health-giving properties of booze—they're mostly either decrepit or wall-eyed.

1900

Pouring it through a funnel doesn't make it medicine,
but you can't blame the old boy for trying.

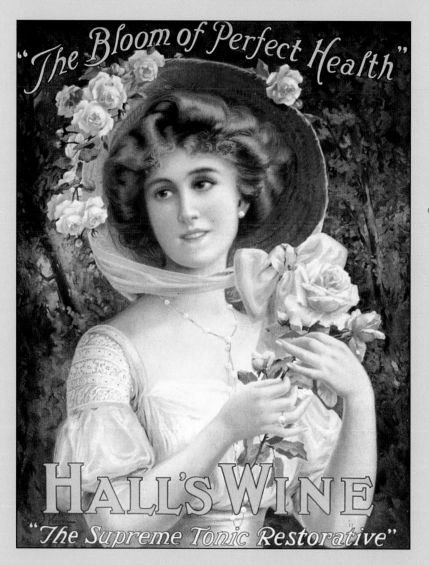

"The Bloom of Perfect Health"

HALL'S WINE

"The Supreme Tonic Restorative"

1910s

This ad might have a fair enough claim if it wasn't for her cross eyes.

1920s

An apple a day keeps the doctor away. And apparently the same is true if it's an alcoholic apple. How convenient!

1930s

Wonder if there's a similar cure for bird flu? Fingers crossed!

1900s

Mason's essence is non-alcoholic, which is just as well if you serve it at kids' parties by the gallon.

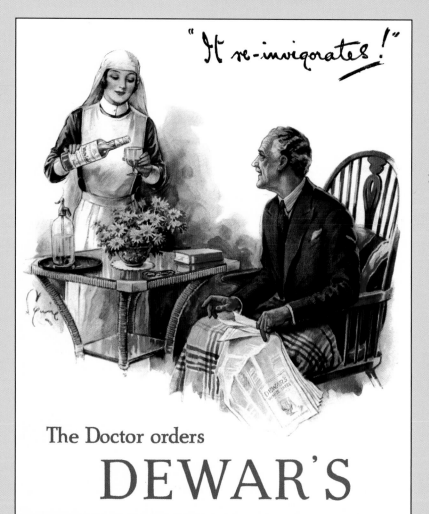

1933

Now that's the kind
of doctor's advice
I like!

1950s

After drinking a mixture of egg and wine, swinging her around like that might not be the best idea.

1958

Miss Rheingold loves a beer before she jumps in her car. Just hope that dog moves out of the way quickly enough.

DRUNKENNESS CURED.

It is now within the reach of Every Woman to Save the Drunkard—A Free Trial Package of a Marvellous Home Remedy Posted to All Who Write for it.

Can be Given in Tea, Coffee, or Food, thus absolutely and secretly Curing the Patient in a Short Time without his knowledge.

There is a cure for drunkenness which has shed a radiance into thousands of hitherto desolate firesides. It does its work so silently and surely that while the devoted wife, sister, or daughter looks on, the drunkard is reclaimed even against his will and without his knowledge or co-operation. The Company who have this grand remedy will send a sample free to all who will write for it. Enough of this remedy is posted in this way to show how it is used in tea, coffee, or food, and that it will cure the dreaded habit quietly and permanently.

A lady residing in Manchester used the remedy as described above, and her experience, told in her own words, will quite likely interest all women deeply. Mrs.—— says: "Yes, I used Antidipso without my husband's knowledge, and completely cured him. He was a hard drinker, a good man when sober, but for years I lived in fear and dread, shame and despair, poverty and disgrace. How shall I tell other women about it? Is it not a wonderful thing that a woman can take matters in her own hands and stamp out this dreadful curse to the home? I am glad you are going to publish my experience, for then I know it will reach hundreds of other poor souls, and they will cure their husbands just as I cured mine. I am so grateful for the marvellous changes that have come into my life that I just feel I would do anything to let every wife and mother know what a blessing Antidipso is. I honestly believe it will cure any drunkard, no matter how far down he may have fallen.—Faithfully yours, Mrs.——."
(Full address sent to *bona-fide* applicants.)

Hundreds of others are reported, even the worst cases where the habit seems to have blotted out the last remaining spark of self-respect. Tears and prayers are of no use. Pleading, pledges, loss of social or business position are unavailing to stem the tide of absolute depravity.

This famous remedy has reunited thousands of scattered families; it has saved thousands of men to social and business prominence and public respect; has guided many a young man into the right road to fortune; has saved the father, the brother, the son, and in many cases the wife and daughter, too. Such a godsend to the home should be known to everyone. Upon application to the **Ward Chemical Co., 10, Century House, Regent Street, London, W.,** they will post a free package of the remedy to you, securely sealed in a plain wrapper, also full directions how to use it, books, testimonials from hundreds who have been cured, and everything needed to aid you in saving those near and dear to you from a life of degradation and ultimate poverty and disgrace. Send for a free trial to-day. It will brighten the rest of your life.

1890s

And if you're still not convinced that drink is good for your health, here's a remedy. Just slip this stuff in his tea and watch him jump back on that wagon!

You too can look like a model

Inner beauty is for ugly people. It's a superficial world we live in so if you want to make the most of what nature gave you, then take a look at the informative ads that follow. Yes, certain gorgeousness awaits you once you've strapped one of these not-at-all-cumbersome contraptions around your head, or smothered your face with one of these categorically non-poisonous lotions, or swallowed a few of these oh-so-tasty-sounding tablets. Want to lose weight? Beef up your muscles? Grow some hair? Not a problem; it's all easily within your reach if you just send a prompt check to the address given …

1900s

Aah, is there a more lovely sight in the world than a little baby clutching a razor blade?

CURVES OF YOUTH

will be yours if you will

"Pull the Cords"

Gives the Flesh the Resiliency and Freshness of Youth

Prevents Double Chins

Effaces Double Chins

PROF. MACK'S

Chin Reducer
and
Beautifier

Reduces Enlarged Glands

The only mechanism producing a concentrated, continuous massage of the chin and neck, dispelling flabbiness of the neck and throat, restoring a rounded contour to thin, scrawny necks and faces, bringing a natural, healthy color to the cheeks, effacing lines and wrinkles. Price only $10. What better investment could be made? Sent postpaid immediately.

Free Booklet

—giving valuable information on how to treat double chin and enhance facial beauty will be sent on request. Write at once to

Prof. Eugene Mack
507 Fifth Ave.   **Suite 1004**   **New York**

1890s

Much as this looks like a torture device, it is actually the secret to a youthful look. A youthful horse, that is.

1890s

Hannibal Lecter has nothing on Madame Rowley. Yet apparently the Toilet Mask "cannot be detected by the closest scrutiny." Unless you happen to notice the huge straps covering her head and the weird skin, of course.

1886

''I love it mommy, but can't I get the push-up bra
version?''

1900s

It's always a worry that you'll put on your night cream and wake up with a flowing beard. But fortunately for this lady, Jonteel "will not grow hair on the face." Phew!

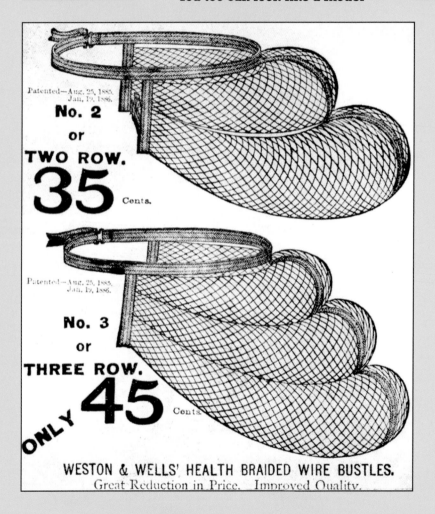

1880

The 19th-century J-Lo wannabe knew just how to create that bootylicious look—just strap a couple of industrial-size sieves to her butt.

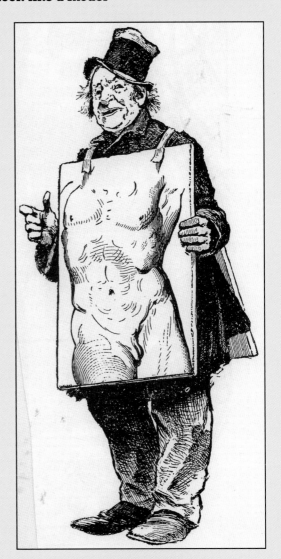

1890s

The back of this
sandwich board
would have shown
whichever fitness-
giving product was
supposed to
provide the
toned physique
on the front.
Of course, the
other possibility is
that he's trying to
con long-sighted,
horny passers-by.

1900s

It's slightly
unnerving when
a product has to
tell you it won't
poison you.

FAT FOLK

Should take **FELL'S REDUCING TABLETS.**

Registered by Government.

A Remarkable Remedy

That Reduces Weight 28 lb. a month.

Every person who is suffering from too much fat can easily be reduced in weight by this new and remarkable remedy that quickly removes all superfluous fat in either sex at the rate of **7 LB. A WEEK.**

It is guaranteed to **Reduce Weight a Pound a Day** without the slightest inconvenience. Do not be afraid of evil consequences. It is a vegetable treatment, is perfectly safe, and gives such a degree of comfort as to astonish those who have panted and perspired under the weight of excessive fat. It improves the breathing, gives the heart freedom, takes off the big stomach, enables the lungs to expand naturally, and **you feel a hundred times better** the first day you try this wonderful **HOME TREATMENT.**

"Getting Fleshier Every Day."

Lost 40 lb. Lady —— writes: "Since taking your tablets I am reduced in weight 40 lb.

Thousands of Testimonials sent on request.

FREE Just to prove how effective, pleasant, and safe this remedy is to reduce weight, we are sending free trials. If you want one send us your name and address and two stamps to pay for postage. It costs you nothing to try it. Each box is sent in a plain sealed package, with no advertisement on it to indicate what it contains. Correspondence strictly confidential. **Address: Fell Formula Association, 20 Century House, Regent Street, London, W.**

1903

This reducing tab "takes off the big stomach," says the small type. Perhaps Ryvita might like to borrow that promise?

YES!
DRI-POO
Certainly Improves My Hair!
Have you tried it yet?

The New Way to Fluff and Clean the Hair

DRI-POO is a delightful preparation and so good for the hair. Excess oil, dandruff, "dirt" and all foreign matter instantly respond to a Dri-Poo treatment. Use it as often as you wish. It is harmless. Just loosen the hair with your fingers, fill with Dri-Poo and brush out. That's all. And the result is hair sweetly clean, fluffy and in the best dressing condition.

We will send a small size can of Dri-Poo to your home postpaid for 25 cents or 50 cents for the large size, if you will mention the name of your merchant.

Our booklet, "The Crown of Beauty," which we will send free on request for the name of your merchant, tells how to prevent discolored, faded, brittle and falling hair, and also gives valuable hints about dressing the hair.

J. J. WITTWER   Seattle. Wash.

1920s

Oh dear, this is an unfortunate name. Or maybe it's not and they really are suggesting rubbing desiccated s**t in your hair.

1920s

This man is frightening. Do not send him your address. No hair is worth it.

For 1940 —
Be Fit & Slim

Every woman wants to look better, to feel better in the year ahead. Slenderness is the way to health, beauty and fitness. A couple of Bile Beans taken nightly enables you to 'slim while you sleep'— surely and safely.

These fine vegetable pills do more than disperse unwanted fat— they purify and enrich the blood, tone up the entire system and make you feel better in health in every way.

So start with Bile Beans to-night and make sure of looking and feeling your best in 1940.

By Taking

BILE BEANS

BRAND PILLS

SOLD EVERYWHERE

1940s

Mmm … bile beans. How very tempting. And if they repeat on you, they'll taste exactly the same.

1940s

Thanks for that, Gil. Looks a little bit like you've just drawn two made-up pictures – one skinny and one beefy – but I'm sure that's not the case.

1947

"If I close my eyes tight enough, mom might stop giving me skin cancer."

1970s

Transformation indeed! She's not only changed from "fat and lonely" to "slim and desirable," she's also gained a third dimension and no longer resembles Chewbacca.

Smoking is good for you

Smoking gets a bad rap these days, what with lung cancer, the hacking cough and the bad breath ... Not so in the late 19th and early 20th centuries. Back then, cigarettes were everyone's best friends. Doctors, dentists, sportsmen, singers and film stars were lining up to lend their names to the cigarette companies' ad campaigns. Each brand was keen to stress that its cigarettes were the ones to relieve your hoarse voice, ward you off from binge eating and stop your teeth from going brown. When ads featured glamorous women, hunky men and kindly old doctors, who wouldn't be convinced?

JOY'S CIGARETTES afford immediate relief in cases of **ASTHMA, WHEEZING, AND WINTER COUGH,** and a little perseverance will effect a permanent cure. Universally recommended by the most eminent physicians and medical authors. Agreeable to use, certain in their effects, and harmless in their action, they may be safely smoked by ladies and children.

All Chemists and Stores, box of 35, 2s. 6d., or post free from WILCOX & Co., 239, OXFORD STREET, LONDON, W.

1890s

You might think a child with asthma needs an inhaler, but apparently not—Joy's cigarettes were great for kids!

1880s

How sweet. Nicotine-addicted babies. Unfortunately, having such an adult taste for tobacco seems to have caused slight premature ageing in this pair— they look like 60-year-old men in dresses!

1910s

Ah, those were the days, when doctors recommended not just 5-a-day of your fruit and veg but also 20-a-day of his favorite smokes.

What the Doctor Smokes

The doctor's choice in tobacco is CRAVEN Mixture, and he is supported in that choice by the verdict of the greatest medical journal in the world—

"The Lancet"

which published on August 24th, 1912, an analytical report showing that of all well-known tobaccos CRAVEN is unmistakably the purest and best, the smoke of other well-known tobaccos yielding **7 to 10 times, and some tobaccos 16 times, as much nicotine** as that found in CRAVEN. Therefore the doctor smokes and should recommend CRAVEN Mixture as the **best** for **health.**

The purity and sweetness of CRAVEN are due to the special process possessed only by Carreras, Ltd., and by which all impurities and crude nicotine are removed.

CRAVEN MIXTURE is made under the same formula as when immortalised by J. M. Barrie as "Arcadia" in my "Lady Nicotine," and it contains nothing but pure tobacco.

On sale all over the world. In cartridges or loose in tins 2oz. 1/3
CARRERAS, LTD. (Est. 1788), Arcadia Works, City Rd., London, E.C.
& Montreal, Canada. West-end Depot : 7, Wardour St. Leicester Sq. London, W.

1900

Cigars are traditionally smoked at the birth of a baby. Not by the baby himself on his 10th birthday.

1930s

Sex sells. And, er, so do doctors by the sound of it.

Her Singing Coach Advised A Light Smoke

CAROLE LOMBARD* PREFERS LUCKIES BECAUSE THEY'RE EASIER ON HER THROAT

"When I had to sing in a recent picture," says Carole Lombard, "I considered giving up smoking. But my voice teacher said I needn't if I'd select a light smoke—Luckies.

"I soon found that even when singing and acting 12 hours a day, I can smoke as many Luckies as I like . . . without the slightest throat irritation."

The reason Luckies are easy on Miss Lombard's throat is because the process "It's Toasted" takes out certain throat irritants found in all tobacco—even the finest.

And Luckies do use the finest tobacco. Sworn records show that among independent tobacco experts—auctioneers, buyers, warehousemen, etc.—Lucky Strike has twice as many exclusive smokers as have all other cigarettes combined.

In the honest judgment of those who spend their lives buying, selling and handling tobacco...with men who know tobacco best . . . it's Luckies—2 to 1.

*Star of the new Paramount production "True Confession"

A Light Smoke

EASY ON YOUR THROAT—"IT'S TOASTED"

LUCKY STRIKE CIGARETTES

WITH TOBACCO EXPERTS... WITH MEN WHO KNOW TOBACCO BEST *It's Luckies 2 to 1*

1930s

What the ad doesn't mention is that Carole is singing baritone in a barbershop quartet.

1932

It's important for a company to identify its target market—Murad obviously thought its was "careless drivers who don't like confrontation." Seems a little narrow, but doesn't Murad know best?

1930s

Don't you just hate the man who dares to cough when surrounded by smokers? How rude!

1930s

Who'd have thought that snacking between meals was the downfall of this aspiring hurdler? If only he'd had a 40-a-day habit.

1910

A lesser known side-effect of chewing tobacco
appears to be loss of bones in the lower limbs.

1940s

Perhaps the most worrying question is whether all those doctors passed along free samples. And what is the doctor with the microscope looking at? Did that particular patient's test results reveal insides turned to ash?

Every doctor in private practice was asked:
—family physicians, surgeons, specialists...
doctors in every branch of medicine—
"What cigarette do you smoke?"

According to a recent Nationwide survey:

More Doctors
Smoke Camels

than any other cigarette!

R. J. Reynolds Tobacco Company, Winston-Salem, N. C.

THE "T-ZONE" TEST WILL TELL YOU

The "T-Zone"—T for taste and T for throat—is your own laboratory, your proving ground, for any cigarette. For only your taste and your throat can decide which cigarette tastes best to you... and how it affects your throat. On the basis of the experience of many, many millions of smokers, we believe Camels will suit your "T-Zone" to a "T."

CAMEL
TURKISH & DOMESTIC BLEND CIGARETTES

Not a guess, not just a trend...but an actual fact based on the statements of doctors themselves to 3 nationally known independent research organizations.

Yes, your doctor was asked...along with thousands and thousands of other doctors from Maine to California. And they've named their choice—the brand that more doctors named as their smoke is *Camel!* Three nationally known independent research organizations found this to be a fact.

Nothing unusual about it. Doctors smoke for pleasure just like the rest of us. They appreciate, just as you, a mildness that's cool and easy on the throat. They too enjoy the full, rich flavor of expertly blended costlier tobaccos. And they named Camels...more of them named Camels than any other brand. Next time you buy cigarettes, try Camels.

1940s

If Fred's 30-day mildness test convinced him, that's good enough for his glamorous assistant!

1940s

Never? Perhaps they mean stain them *white*.

1930s

Bonfires might be the usual means of generating Native American smoke signals, but cigarettes are certainly easier to fit in your pocket.

1940

Sports stars usually endorse boring things like isotonic drinks, but not Fred Perry—his pre-match routine is a lot less dull!

STRAMONIUM CIGARETTES HELPFUL IN ASTHMA

as reported in the British
Medical Journal, August 15, 1959

**Noted allergist reinvestigates
an old treatment for bronchial asthma**

For about 150 years Europeans have inhaled smoke from burning stramonium leaves to relieve asthmatic attacks.

Now a noted allergist reports in the British Medical Journal that results of controlled studies leave no doubt that inhaling stramonium (atropine*) smoke has a beneficial effect on the function of the lungs in bronchial obstruction.

The results indicate that smoking stramonium cigarettes has a definite place in the treatment of asthma, increasing the vital capacity and giving a feeling of relief, without unpleasant side effects. In many cases during the controlled study the patients voluntarily commented on their increased ease of breathing.

Stramonium cigarettes have been manufactured by R. Schiffmann Co. for more than 80 years and have been *available without prescription in every drug store* throughout the U. S. and Canada under the name of ASTHMADOR. These cigarettes contain no tobacco and are not habit forming.

ASTHMADOR is also sold in pipe mixture or as aromatic incense powder. Sufferers from bronchial asthma will almost invariably find relief, as indicated in this report.

*Atropine
is the
alkaloid of
stramonium.

1960s

Stramonium is now known to be toxic—surely being poisoned would be classed as an "unpleasant side effect!"

Blow in her face and she'll follow you anywhere.

Hit her with tangy Tipalet Cherry. Or rich, grape-y Tipalet Burgundy. Or luscious Tipalet Blueberry. It's Wild! Tipalet. It's new. Different. Delicious in taste and in aroma. A puff in her direction and she'll follow you, anywhere. Oh yes... you get smoking satisfaction without inhaling smoke.

Smokers of America, do yourself a flavor. Make your next cigarette a **Tipalet.**

New from Muriel.   About 5 for 25¢.

1975

An unusual flirting technique, this one. Or perhaps that's chloroform he's blowing at her and she'll be out in seconds?

You are what you eat: a donut

Healthy eating is nothing new. It's just that back in the first half of the 20th century, "healthy eating" meant stuffing your face with sweets and fizzy drinks—hooray! Sounds like much more fun than boring old fruit and vegetables.

But while a lot of these brands are healthy-enough foods that are still going strong today, their advertising has grown up a lot in the last 70 or so years – you won't see many happy porcine-shaped people or sad and raggedy-looking urchins in modern ads, more's the pity.

1890s

In the 1890s, being as fat as a pig was obviously something to be envied. Why isn't that the case any more, alas?

1563

This painting, *Summer* by Guiseppi Arcimbaldo, has been used for countless commercials, as if having a cabbage head and a zucchini for a nose are things to aspire to.

FEBRUARY 18, 1911]   *THE SPHERE*   ix

Which of these Two Children do you think is nourished with OAT-FOODS ?

How much of the difference between these children is due to Oat-Food has been proved by the National Food Enquiry Bureau, which has just canvassed hundreds of homes— homes where live children like these—the strong and happy, the weak and hopeless.

The Investigators have gone to homes in slum districts throughout Great Britain where are bred the anæmic, the incapable, the undeveloped. In those sections Oat-Food is comparatively unknown.

They have carefully investigated the schools. In one Birmingham school, 88 out of 100 better-class pupils use Oat-Food. In the congested districts of London, *only 3 in 100 are regular users.*

Only 3 in 100 Poor Homes.

Think of it! Only 3 in 100 get the most nourishing and most economical food!

In speaking of one poor family (in Leeds) which *eats* Oat-Food, the Report of the National Food Enquiry Bureau says: "Good, healthy, clear-eyed, rosy-cheeked children." On the same Investigation Sheet six children, *who never get Oat-Food*, are described as : "One child consumptive ; five anæmic."

On the other hand, a canvass of high-class homes shows that 75 out of 100 use Oat-Food ; and the parents in these homes report the great benefit their children derive from the Oat-Food diet.

In 50 per cent. of the workhouses investigated there are not 3 in 100 of the inmates who had the advantage of Oat-Food in their youth.

In Good Class—90 in 100.

At the famous universities and public schools, an average of 90 out of 100 of the athletes were " brought up on " Oat-Food, and the proportion of those who use Oat-Foods in " training " is 10 to 1.

The Investigation's Report shows that out of 514 doctors (in general practice, educational doctors and medical officers of health), 494 declare that an increased consumption of Oat-Food would greatly benefit the nation (only 9 say " No " ; 11 have no decided opinion).

The doctors say so because they know that for your money you get in oats a more perfect combination of carbohydrates, more proteids, organic phosphorus, and lecithin than in any other food.

Carbohydrates are the heat and energy-giving elements of food, proteid is the body-building part of food. Phosphorus is the brain-food ; lecithin the food of the nerves and nerve-centres.

Oat-Food at its Best.

The whole world knows that Oat-Food is found at its best in Quaker Oats.

The large, thin flakes that cook and digest so easily— The delicious flavour impossible to any other Oat-Food—

The purity and cleanliness of Quaker Oats—never touched by hand through all the unique process of milling—Sold SEALED.

The Economy proved by " 40 Meals for Sixpence."— These are a few of the reasons why Quaker Oats is

The one Perfect Oat-Food

Quaker Oats

The food that builds brains and bodies

The Greatest of Food Reformers.

Through the courtesy of the Bureau we can send a copy of the Report to you if you are interested. Address, Quaker Oats Ltd., Dept. 308, 11, Finsbury Square, London, E.C.

The Greatest of Foods is sold only in this sealed packet.

1911

The dirty, scraggy-looking one on the left or the goblin-ears child on the right?

1890s

Man alive! Was the 19th-century housewife so strong she could crush a whole pig?! In that case, you can see how she'd get away with serving what looks like one gross pie—who'd be brave enough to refuse to eat it?

1920s

Well? Do you?
Best have another
Kit Kat or Chunky,
just to be on the
safe side.

---

108   THE SATURDAY EVENING POST   October 27, 1928

Do you eat enough candy?

See what the modern authorities say about candy in the diet — why and how you should eat it

CANDY IS A FOOD! that's the first thing to know about it. Candy supplies definite needs of the body, just like milk, fruit, vegetables, cereals. Candy, in fact, furnishes several vital elements of the diet, without which you couldn't keep well!

So this is the word of modern dietary science—eat candy sensibly, eat it as a food—if you do this you will get the greatest possible enjoyment and benefit from it.

How candy fills important bodily needs

Candy is sometimes considered as an energy food only, because it is so remarkable in that respect. But candy is much more than that. In the candy shown on this page, for example, you will find: Proteins, carbohydrates, fats, mineral salts, and vitamins—all vital to health.

You doubtless recall having read that Gertrude Ederle ate candy for "body fuel" when she swam the channel, that soldiers, athletes and explorers use it for the same purpose.

Considered as a source of quick energy for the body—an extremely necessary food-function—candy is a near perfect food. Considered as a complex food, the source of regulative and building elements (proteins, vitamins and mineral salts) candy also has a place in the properly balanced diet.

Caroline Hunt,* noted specialist in Home Economics, has therefore recommended that candy be made a part of the "sweets" ration, which consists of about five pounds a week for the family of five. Candy may constitute whatever part of this is desired.

*Specialist in Home Economics, U. S. Dept. of Agriculture, Farmer's Bulletin Number 1313.

SWEETEN THE DAY WITH CANDY

Hallowe'en comes on October 31, the eve of All Saints' Day, an occasion for happy parties. Candy is always part of the picture.

A hint to women (and men, too) who want to be thinner

Contrary to the old superstition, candy has no unique fat-producing qualities. Such authorities as Gordon and von Stanley** even suggest the use of candy in a slenderizing diet.

Here is a suggestion: eat candy as a dessert, as often as you find it agreeable. Let it take the place of the heavy, rich desserts, which are difficult to "burn" as fuel, and which tend more to be converted into tissue-fat.

**American Journal of the Medical Sciences—Jan., 1928

Candy thus supplies the need of a sweet after meals in the most wholesome way. Serve it alone or with fruits and nuts.

How to use candy as a food

Treat candy exactly like other foods! The best diet is a *varied* diet and a *balanced* diet. Don't try to live on any one or half-dozen foods. Even milk alone, the most nearly perfect of all foods, is not enough in itself to keep you in good health. Don't make a meal of milk, or potatoes, or fruits alone—or candy! See that *all* the necessary elements are there in proper proportion.

Divide your food-budget like this, for example:

*"About one fifth for vegetables and fruits
About one fifth for milk and cheese
About one fifth for meats, fish and eggs
About one fifth for breads and cereals
About one fifth for fats and sugar (candy)"*

(Cited by Dr. Henry C. Sherman, "Chemistry of Food and Nutrition," MacMillan.)

A book for you

Dr. Herman N. Bundesen has written a scientific, modern booklet in everyday language for you—called "The New Knowledge of Candy." Beautifully printed and illustrated in colors. Use the coupon below, and send ten cents.

Please send me Dr. Bundesen's Book on Candy. Ten cents enclosed.

Name _____

Address _____

ABOVE STATEMENTS APPROVED BY DR. HERMAN N. BUNDESEN

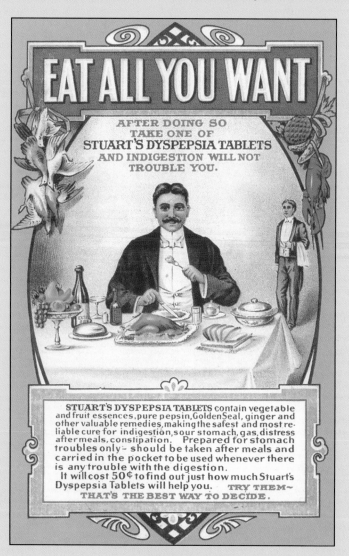

EAT ALL YOU WANT

AFTER DOING SO
TAKE ONE OF
STUART'S DYSPEPSIA TABLETS
AND INDIGESTION WILL NOT
TROUBLE YOU.

STUART'S DYSPEPSIA TABLETS contain vegetable and fruit essences, pure pepsin, Golden Seal, ginger and other valuable remedies, making the safest and most reliable cure for indigestion, sour stomach, gas, distress after meals, constipation.   Prepared for stomach troubles only— should be taken after meals and carried in the pocket to be used whenever there is any trouble with the digestion.
It will cost 50¢ to find out just how much Stuart's Dyspepsia Tablets will help you.   TRY THEM~
THAT'S THE BEST WAY TO DECIDE.

1910s

Indigestion may not trouble you, but the massive gut you'll get if you "eat all you want" just might.

1930s

Gee whiz, how fun is breakfast in this house? I'm guessing it's not the sauerkraut flavor that he's drinking, or he wouldn't look nearly so happy.

1940s

The host of the 1940s had it right—why slave over a hot stove when you can buy your dinner in a sack?

1942

This guy loves his sausage sandwich! Plus eating sausages to defeat Hitler sounds a lot easier than the other option.

FOOD POWER will help Win the War

Sausage is FOOD POWER!

FOOD POWER BUILDS MAN POWER to do a war winning job. Eat for Food Power because the "U. S. Wants Us Strong." Follow Uncle Sam's Nutrition Program. Every day eat meat, poultry or fish, fruit, vegetables, bread, cereal, milk, cheese, butter or other spreads. These foods contain Food Power . . . and sausage and SKINLESS frankfurters are concentrated meat foods that are delicious and good for you. They contain vitamins, complete

proteins, carbohydrates and minerals. 100% edible . . . no waste . . . easy to fix . . . help meal planning.

THERE ARE MANY KINDS OF SAUSAGE, SKINLESS frankfurters and wieners. Each with its own appetizing flavor and goodness in sandwiches, cold and hot meals. Leading packers now protect the food value and flavor of sausage in clear, sparkling "VISKING" casings . . . a cellulose covering

you'll recognize instantly. However, the "VISKING" casings are removed from SKINLESS frankfurters and wieners. The surface you see is formed by the wiener itself in the smoking process.

YOUR DEALER KNOWS SAUSAGE, SKINLESS frankfurters and wieners. His stock includes many kinds and brands to fit your needs. Buy wisely so that your meals will always have "Food Power."

U.S. NEEDS US STRONG

THIS TYPE OF FOOD IS AMONG THOSE RECOMMENDED IN THE NUTRITION FOOD RULES

EAT NUTRITIONAL FOOD

SERVE THIS NUTRITIONAL MEAL MADE WITH

Skinless
TRADE MARK
FRANKFURTERS OR WIENERS

. . . creamed carrot casserole and deviled eggs. Include other foods recommended in the U. S. Nutrition Program.

Having no skins, SKINLESS frankfurters and wieners cook quickly, don't split open to lose their food value and flavory juices.

NO SKINS! Stripped for Action!

THE VISKING CORPORATION • 6733 WEST 65TH STREET, CHICAGO, ILLINOIS

"VISKING" is the registered trade mark of The Visking Corporation   Copyright 1942, The Visking Corporation

1950s

Yes, that's right, mom's fed up of looking after you so it's nothing but peas from now on.

1950s

Personally, I use up my "can do" sitting in front of old *Friends* re-runs, but it's good to know I'm replacing lost energy and not just stuffing my face with chocolate.

THE "CRAVE for CANDY"... is a call for energy

America Loves Candy   *America Needs Energy*

Ever wonder why candy tastes so especially good when you've taken some out-of-the-ordinary exercise?

The answer is—

You've burnt up energy; you need an energy refuel.

That's the fundamental story of candy—quick energy for bodies that need energy; more "Can Do" for the person who has temporarily used up his "Can Do."

By yourself or with other folks, is there any more pleasant way of restoring energy than through candy—box, bar or bagful?

Candy Is Delicious Food

CANDY'S DANDY...KEEP IT HANDY

COUNCIL ON CANDY of the NATIONAL CONFECTIONERS' ASSOCIATION
Headquarters: One North LaSalle Street, Chicago 2, Illinois
...an organization devoted to the dissemination of authoritative information about candy.

1950s

This child doesn't look convinced by the pesticide-covered juice, but maybe she's just mesmerized by her mother's magnificent eyebrows.

How chemistry is saving your orange juice!

Last summer an invasion of the Mediterranean Fruit Fly threatened to destroy Florida's huge citrus crop. Prompt action in spraying thousands of acres with malathion, the remarkably versatile insecticide developed by American Cyanamid Company, is achieving control. As a result, millions of dollars worth of citrus fruits and juices are being saved for America's breakfast table! Here is a dramatic example of how Cyanamid's chemical developments are helping the farmer protect and increase our nation's crops—to serve and conserve in making the fullest possible use of the country's agricultural resources. AMERICAN CYANAMID COMPANY, 30 Rockefeller Plaza, New York 20, N.Y.

CYANAMID

1900s

All this eating can play havoc with a girl's digestion. But never fear, Beecham's laxatives will sort things out, leaving you with that attractive, easygoing look.

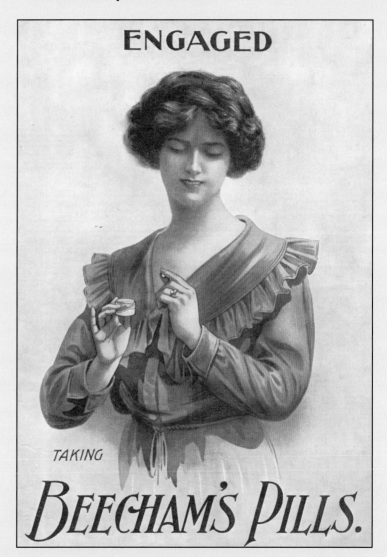

Miracle cures

Feeling a bit down in the dumps? Lacking in vital energy? Then look no further than your nearest plug socket. Yes, back when electricity was new and exciting, consumers were clamoring to buy the latest belt, brush, or appliance that would perk them up. Nothing revitalizes quite like an electric shock.

Perhaps the greatest example of gullibility seen in these miracle cures is whoever seriously believed that the horse exercise machine was an innocent home workout. Not that it always cheered up its riders. Laconic Calvin Coolidge used the mechanical horse for exercise during his White House days.

1880s

No need to backcomb your hair with this little beauty; use the electric brush and watch your hair stand on end.

1890s

Wonderful discovery! Wear this magnet to get rid of "impure blood." Warning: side effects include clothes falling off.

1890s

"Oh, this is so
exciting, having my
portrait painted …
What did you say
I'll be advertising?"

HARNESS' EYE BATTERY

(PATENTED).

THE "WONDER CURE" OF THE 19th CENTURY.

A MARVELLOUS INVENTION.

AWAY WITH EYE-GLASSES AND EYE LOTIONS.

PRICE

12s. 6d.

POST FREE.

By the use of this simple instrument, all the horrible experiences of Leeching, Bleeding, and Surgical Operations are entirely obviated.

Away with Leeching, Bleeding, and Surgical Operations.

PRICE

12s. 6d.

POST FREE.

A NEW and PAINLESS method of promptly curing all diseases of the Eye, and defective eyesight. Call at 52, **OXFORD STREET, LONDON, W.,** and test the instrument for yourself, free of charge.

HARNESS' BATTERY

CURES WEAK EYES RESTORES FAILING SIGHT

52, OXFORD ST LONDON W.

REDUCED FAC-SIMILE OF HARNESS' EYE-BATTERY. WILL LAST FOR EVER

HARNESS' EYE BATTERY is perfectly safe to use, even by children of tender years, the application being entirely under the patient's control.

HARNESS' EYE BATTERY, in addition to PREVENTING and CURING DISEASES OF THE EYE, will cure asthenopia, and **POSITIVELY RESTORES WEAKNESS OF VISION,** whether resulting from advancing age, or from that general nervous prostration which prejudicially affects the optic nerve. It also speedily **CURES SPECKS BEFORE THE EYES** (*Muscæ Volitantes*), so generally complained of, by those suffering from early excesses and in a low and nervous state. Such patients will find in HARNESS' EYE BATTERY an absolute remedy for the malady, which is a real and not, as supposed, an imaginary one, and shows undoubted local manifestation of a debilitated state.

PAMPHLET POST-FREE.

EYES

SUCCESSFULLY TREATED.

HARNESS' EYE BATTERY, is admitted to exercise a rapid influence upon the complex system of nerves, blood-vessels, fluids, and membranes constituting the most wonderful of Nature's mysterious mechanisms. Almost every disease of the eye can now be successfully treated by the systematic use (according to directions) of HARNESS' EYE BATTERY, which can be applied at any time, as is sufficiently portable to be conveniently carried in the pocket, and may be used by any person from infancy to old age, with perfect safety.

Stated simply, this is a system of curing diseases and weakness of the eye, and restoring normal acuteness of vision by assisting Nature, through influencing the circulatory functions to convey to the affected region a sufficient supply of healthy blood, and thus to annihilate the morbid and stagnant conditions which foster and maintain disease.

HARNESS' EYE BATTERY is sent, carefully packed, with directions for using it, post-free, on receipt of 12s. 6d.

The Medical Battery Co., Ld., **52, OXFORD St., LONDON, W.**

1890s

No more sticking leeches on your eyes. In that case, even an eye battery sounds like a good idea.

1890s

Brain Salt promises a certain cure for "excessive study." Another is *American Idol.*

CURES
HEADACHES
AND
INDIGESTION

EFFERVESCENT

BRAIN

F. Newbery & Son

SALT

(TITLE REGISTERED)   PRICE 2/9 PER BOTTLE
A POSITIVE RELIEF AND CURE FOR
Brain Troubles, Headaches
Sea Sickness,
Nervous Debility, Sleeplessness, Excessive Study, Mania, Over Brainwork,
etc etc.
F. NEWBERY & SONS.
1 and 3 King Edward St. London, E.C.
TRADE MARK REGISTERED IN U.S. BY F. NEWBERY & SONS, FEB 10, 1888

HORSE EXERCISE AT HOME.

By Royal Letters Patent

Vigor's Horse-Action Saddle

PERSONALLY ORDERED BY
H. R. H. THE PRINCESS OF WALES.

Her Excellency the Countess of Aberdeen *writes:* "That the Saddle has given her complete satisfaction."

The *ADVANTAGES* of this *UNIQUE SUBSTITUTE* för Horse-Riding are:

It promotes health in the same degree that Horse-Riding does.

It invigorates the system by bringing all the **VITAL ORGANS** into **INSPIRITING ACTION.**

It acts directly upon the **CIRCULATION,** and prevents **STAGNATION OF THE LIVER.**

It is a complete cure for **OBESITY, HYSTERIA,** and **GOUT.**

TROT, CANTER, & GALLOP.

VIGOR LONDON

LANCET:—"Both the expense and difficulty of riding on a live horse are avoided. The invention is very ingenious."

FIELD:—"We have had an opportunity of trying one of the VIGOR's Horse-Action Saddles, and found it very like that of riding on a horse; the same muscles are brought into play as when riding."

WORLD:—"It is good for the figure, good for the complexion, and especially good for the health."

PARTICULARS, TESTIMONIALS, and PRESS OPINIONS POST FREE.

Vigor & Cº 21, Baker Sᵗ, London.

1890s

Ahem. It seems the Countess of Aberdeen is "completely satisfied" by her horse-action saddle. Lucky her.

1900s

This belt apparently provides "courage." Or maybe others are just scared by the constant buzz emanating from your middle.

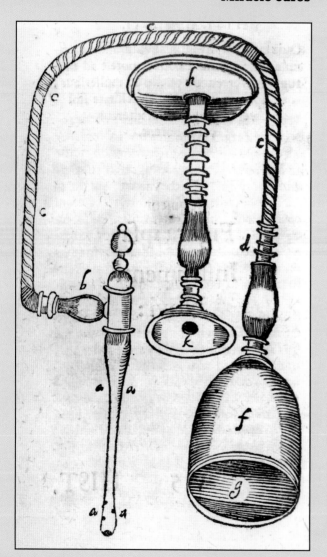

1611

This early ad was for Bartholin's Clyster, a revolutionary enema device that blew smoke up users' backsides. And no, I've no idea which bit goes where either, but that's probably just as well.

Why catch their Influenza?

YOU need not! Just carry Formamint with you and suck these delicious tablets whenever you are in danger of being infected by other people.

"Suck at least four or five a day"—so says Dr. Hopkirk in his standard work "Influenza"—for "in Formamint we possess the best means of preventing the infective processes which, if neglected, may lead to serious complications."

Seeing that such complications often lead to Pneumonia, Bronchitis, and other dangerous diseases, it is surely worth while to protect yourself by this safe, certain, and inexpensive means. Protect the children, too, for their delicate little organisms are very exposed to germ-attack, especially during school-epidemics. Be careful, however, not to confuse Formamint with so-called formalin tablets, but see that it bears the name of the sole manufacturers: Genatosan, Limited (British Purchasers of Sanatogen Co.), 12, Chenies Street, London, W.C.1. (Chairman : The Viscountess Rhondda.)

"Attack the germs before they attack you!"

Though genuine Formamint is scarce your chemist can still obtain it for you at the pre-war price — 2/2 per bottle. Order it to-day.

Formamint
THE GERM KILLING THROAT TABLET

1918

The flu epidemic of 1918 killed millions, but clearly not those sucking Formamint!

1920s

Shock tactics in advertising are nothing new, as this one for windshield glass shows. What's more surprising is that a man could fly through the screen of your father's automobile and receive nothing more serious than "numerous cuts!" What was it made of? Marshmallow?

1920s

Jim was doing well to keep his relaxed and pleasant manner when faced with the terror of sogginess.

ABSOLUTELY CURES
Consumption, Asthma, Bronchitis, and all diseases of the Throat, Lungs and Chest.

A POSITIVE, EFFECTUAL and RADICAL CURE.

WRITE FOR TESTIMONIALS.

Sold by Druggists, or sent on receipt of price, $2.00.

THE ONLY LUNG PAD CO.,
DETROIT, MICH.

1880s

Surely this isn't the ONLY lung pad company? When a piece of merchandise is this convincing, why isn't every company clamoring to sell it?

1890s

Dr Williams is on to a winner here—create a random-sounding tablet, market it to a specific group of people, and—most of all—keep very quiet about what it's supposed to do!

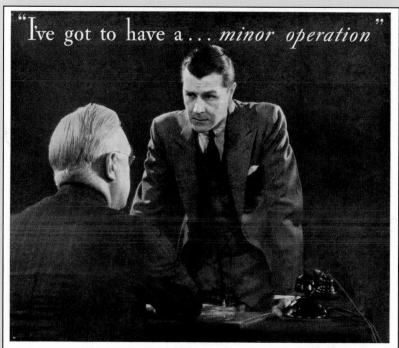

"**I**'ve got to have a ... *minor operation*"

More serious than most men realize...
the troubles caused by harsh toilet tissue

IN nearly every business organization a surprisingly large percentage of the employees are suffering from rectal trouble.

This fact is well known to companies that require physical examinations of their personnel. Yet even these same concerns are frequently negligent in providing equipment that will safeguard the health of their employees.

Harsh toilet tissue, for instance.

Any physician will tell you that mucous membrane can be seriously inflamed by the use of harsh or chemically impure toilet tissue.

Some specialists estimate that 65 per cent of all

men and women at middle age suffer from troubles caused or aggravated by inferior toilet tissue.

Protection from rectal illness is just as important in the home as in business. Fortunately, women are more careful in matters of this kind than men. Already millions of homes are equipped with ScotTissue or Waldorf—the tissues that doctors and hospitals recommend.

Extremely soft, cloth-like and absorbent, these safety tissues cannot harm the most sensitive skin. They are chemically pure, contain no harsh irritants.

Be safe . . . at home, at work. Insist on Scot-Tissue or Waldorf. Scott Paper Company, Chester, Pa. In Canada, Scott Paper Company, Ltd., Toronto, Ontario.

SCOTTISSUE, *an extremely soft, pure white, absorbent roll containing 1,000 sheets*

2 *for* 25¢

Price for U. S. only

Soft as old Linen
ScotTissue
The absorbent soft white Toilet Tissue
Scott Paper Company

WALDORF, *soft and absorbent, yet inexpensive*

Now 6¢ *a roll*

Price for U. S. only

Stores displaying this sign **HEALTH PRODUCTS** *It will pay you to buy in quantities* are featuring Health Products during June and July

1930s

What on earth is he doing with his toilet-paper roll? And are they seriously suggesting you ask your employers to change their brand of toilet tissue?

NOW she is *immune* from 'Flu, Colds or any epidemic for 12 months because she is wearing the Simpson Iodine Locket

Whilst worn, the Iodine is constantly breathed into the system through the skin pores for 12 months (the life of the Locket).

Men wear the Locket in the vest pocket.

More than 2,500,000 wearers have in this way been kept free from 'Flu, Colds, Catarrh and Rheumatism.

This is Mr. J. W. Simpson, Chemist, the Iodine Specialist, Inventor of the "IODOLOK" Iodine Locket.

The Locket is sold by all Chemists, 1/9 each, 3 for 4/6. But see the name and the word "IODOLOK" embossed in gold on the Locket, as there are some cheap imitations about.

J. W. SIMPSON (CHEMIST) LTD., ALDWYCH HOUSE, LONDON, W.C.2

27

A woman's work is always fun

Before the evil cloud of feminism cast its shadow over so many happy homes, encouraging women to leave their housework and wear dungarees instead, little ladies the world over were busy having fun scrubbing clothes and vacuuming. They liked nothing more than to receive a household appliance as a holiday or birthday gift, and serve up a delicious meal of canned soup to their hungry husbands. Occasionally, they even troubled their pretty little heads with the world of work, where they had much fun typing up clever men's business letters (goodness knows what they were all about, but when the girls' typewriters were so nice and colorful, who cared?)

1920s

Moral of the story: wash your panties or lose your job.

A WARNING
to girls who work in offices

Nervous strain increases perspiration—
don't run the risk of "undie odor"

Please do not expect employers or even office mates to warn you of this hard-to-forgive offense.

Girls who work in offices are so apt to run the risk of unpleasant "undie odor." Naturally so, because everybody perspires more under nervous tension. And underthings are constantly absorbing perspiration acids and odors. Others notice this before you do.

Don't take chances that may spoil your business success. There is one sure way to *know* you're fresh and sweet. Lux removes "undie odor" *completely*, yet so gently that colors and fabrics are never harmed.

It's delightfully easy to Lux your lingerie and stockings after *every* wearing. Then you avoid all embarrassment, all risk of offending. This dainty habit takes only 4 minutes, or less!

Try Lux FREE! Try this wonderful care for your lingerie, at our expense. Just send us your name and address, and by return mail you will receive a full-sized package of Lux free. Write today to Lever Brothers Company, Dept. BX-5, Cambridge, Massachusetts.

Risking her job?

Clever, efficient, her loyalty and hard work are surely appreciated. Yet this offense is too serious—no one could overlook it. If only some one could warn her that she is risking her job!

Pretty Hands
Lux in the DISHPAN leaves hands soft, snow-white. Costs only 1c a day!

LUX for underthings—
keeps them like new in spite of frequent washing

1930s

Yes, and the more comments like that a husband makes, the more likely he is to go to work in dirty socks.

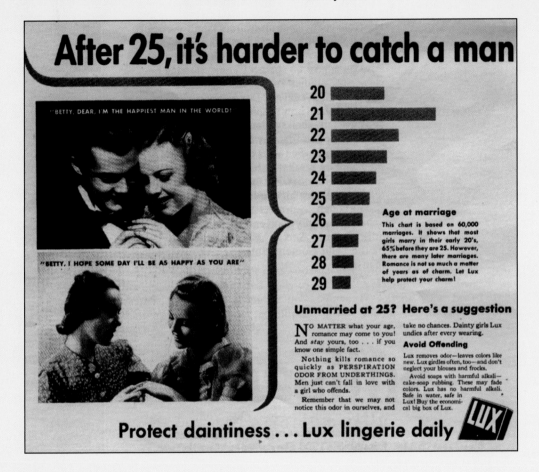

1930s

Got that? Men can't fall in love with a woman who offends!

Clever Wife

she knows that men like soups ···and hearty soups!

Ever notice the look of sunny contentment that comes into a man's face after he has eaten a plate of good hot soup? You might almost call soup the chief aid of anxious wives because it's so certain to be what the man wants to eat first, when he comes home tired and hungry. Something that tastes mighty good, and goes right to the spot—*quick*.

You have just the answer in Campbell's Soups—off the shelf—on the range—in the plate—all in a twinkling. You can tell at the first spoonful he likes it—and how! It has the rich, sparkling flavor that chases his frowns and makes him appreciate you as a "cook." Especially when you select one of those extra-substantial Campbell's Soups which are "naturals" for the male appetite. The suggestions below are sure to help you when you visit your grocer.

1930s

Clever?! For a start she's serving soup on a plate, which is never a good idea.

Soups men like ··· a few *Campbell's* favorites

Oh, Wednesdays and Fridays
Are great nights for me,
With Campbell's broadcasting
Such laughter and glee!

CAMPBELL'S ON THE AIR!

Fridays
Dick Powell's "Hollywood Hotel"
—all-star revue—9-10 P.M. (E.S.T.)
Columbia Network — coast-to-coast.

Wednesdays
George Burns & Gracie Allen
—new program—8:30 P.M. E.S.T.
—7:30 C.S.T.—9:30 M.T.— 8:30 P.S.T.
Columbia Network — coast-to-coast.

NOODLE with chicken —
A feast in "homey" goodness which no man, woman or child can resist. It just teems with chicken richness (broth and meat)—and those fine egg noodles which delight the hunger. Here is an "old-timer" glorified by Campbell's into one of the most popular soups of today. Just taste it!

OX TAIL—
A hit with men—and everyone with a vigorous appetite. It's a richly meaty soup with its own world-famous flavor—yet seldom attempted in the home kitchen. Campbell's bring it to you at its best—selected ox tail joints, invigorating meat broth, nourishing vegetables — deliciously combined.

LOOK FOR THE RED-AND-WHITE LABEL

PEPPER POT—
The real Philadelphia kind, so famous in old Colonial days and ever after. It gives you a splendid chance to vary your soups with a welcome and delightful novelty. Beef broth, macaroni dumplings, meat, potatoes, onion, ground black peppercorns, marjoram, thyme, sweet pimientos—what a soup!

VEGETABLE-BEEF—
The true old-fashioned vegetable soup which contains tempting pieces of meat. You can depend upon it as a sure attraction to the man in the house. It's so hearty and satisfying — so abundantly supplied with meat and vegetables and barley—a meal in itself. And for the children's lunch or supper, nothing could be better!

1936

Poor old stinky Edna. Can you imagine a more horrifying prospect for a woman than being unmarried in her late 20s?

Often a bridesmaid but never a bride

EDNA'S case was really a pathetic one. Like every woman, her primary ambition was to marry. Most of the girls of her set were married—or about to be. Yet not one possessed more grace or charm or loveliness than she.

And as her birthdays crept gradually toward that tragic thirty-mark, marriage seemed farther from her life than ever.

She was often a bridesmaid but never a bride.

*   *   *

That's the insidious thing about halitosis (unpleasant breath). You, yourself, rarely know when you have it. And even your closest friends won't tell you.

Sometimes, of course, halitosis comes from some deep-seated organic disorder that requires professional advice. But usually—and fortunately—halitosis is only a local condition that yields to the regular use of Listerine as a mouth wash and gargle. It is an interesting thing that this well-known antiseptic that has been in use for years for surgical dressings, possesses these unusual properties as a breath deodorant.

It halts food fermentation in the mouth and leaves the breath sweet, fresh and clean. *Not* by substituting some other odor but by really removing the old one. The Listerine odor itself quickly disappears. So the systematic use of Listerine puts you on the safe and polite side.

Your druggist will supply you with Listerine. He sells lots of it. It has dozens of different uses as a safe antiseptic and has been trusted as such for half a century. Remember, Listerine is as safe as it is effective. Lambert Pharmacal Company, St. Louis, Mo.

THE HIT OF PALM BEACH

Fits into purse, keeps powder, lipstick and other cosmetics in one place.

This smart Moire Cosmetic Bag **FREE** →
WITH PURCHASE OF LARGE SIZE **LISTERINE**
This offer good in U.S.A. only

At your druggist's while they last

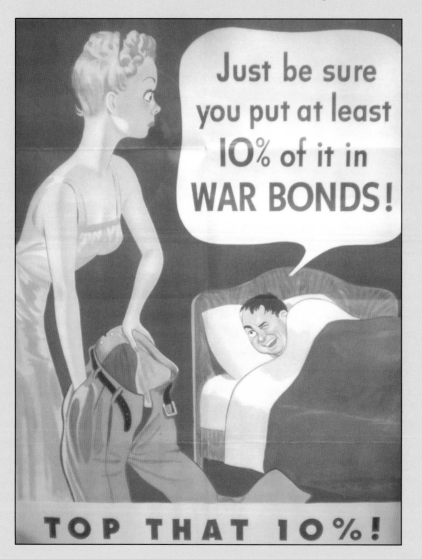

1942

He's an understanding fellow, isn't he? Or maybe he's just resigned to the fact that women are all devious thieves who'll steal anything you leave lying around.

1940s

Now she has her Climax, washday's her favorite day of the week. Funny that.

"Women have been shot for that!"

MR.: Hey, just what are you up to? Grabbing one of my two remaining Arrow shirts for your own, my dear?

MRS.: Well, it looked so nice on you I thought I—

MR.: You did, eh? You thought I wouldn't mind losing that handsome Arrow Collar ...that special Mitoga figure cut...that—

MRS.: Look, Bill! Let's not get *silly!* You've got three or four shirts as it is, and—

MR.: Yes, Fond Wife! But only *two* Arrows! Arrows with that magic San-

forized label, meaning: No Shrinkage Over 1%—If That. Well, my answer is: *"Leave 'em alone!"*

MRS.: Listen—you big clown! *I* don't want your precious Arrow shirt. I wanted it for Eddie, your own son. He's going to some big party tonight, and there's a girl, and the poor kid remembered how you bawled him out for swiping a shirt from you before the war. So I—

MR.: Aw, don't cry, honey. Why didn't you SAY so? Take it. Women are so doggone devious, doggone 'em. Handkerchief? *Cluett, Peabody & Co., Inc.*

ARROW SHIRTS

*$3*25 • *$3*75 • *$3*95 • *$4*75

1950

It's a common advertising trick to feature a happy family the consumer can aspire to. One headed by a raving psychopath, however, is less usual.

1940s

And what makes a perfect man? Someone who pretends to love getting another boring shirt for his birthday?

WHAT MAKES A PERFECT WOMAN?

Do you freeze with him at football matches? Brave the 'jalopy'—and *blow* your nylons? Suffer sock-darning with a smile? Good! You get 7 out of 10. Now go for full marks. (Easy!) Just give him a TERN. Definitely the gift he'll *adore* you for, every time he wears it. (You'll love him in it, too). *Wonderful* shirt. Never needs ironing. Always looks smart. Bliss for bachelors! Ready to give—with your love—for only **39/6.** In white, cream, blue, grey or green never-iron poplin. Buy him a TERN today.

CHRISTMAS TIME—TERN TIME

TERN
Trade Mark *by Consulate*
NEVER-IRON POPLIN
M. Bertish & Co., Ltd. London, N.15.

1950s

Seconds after the blindfold came off, the vacuum cleaner was wrapped around Mr. Smith's head.

To Gladden Hearts and *Lighten* Labor

DOWMETAL···THE WORLD'S LIGHTEST STRUCTURAL ALLOY

Almost a score of years ago Dow undertook to produce American made magnesium alloys—the metal that is a full third lighter than aluminum.

Then, and through the years, Dow looked forward to the day when the startling lightness of this metal would make a myriad of tasks easier for mankind.

First to take advantage of Dowmetal was the aviation industry where its unique lightness combined with strength is of untold value.

Gradually it found acceptance in industry—adding speed to machine parts, cutting power costs, aiding transportation and speeding manual operations.

Finally, a year ago, Dowmetal entered the household appliance field through its adoption by The Hoover Company for the famous Hoover One Fifty Cleaning Ensemble. So audible has been customer enthusiasm for the amazing lightness of that product that Hoover designers determined to incorporate this feature in the just-announced lower priced Hoover Model 25.

Obviously, Dow has long since overcome those problems of production which stood in its developmental period as economic barriers to wider use. Moreover, recent advances in fabrication, notably high speed die-casting, enable users of Dowmetal to adapt it to their production methods on a close-cost basis.

Thus, the ambition for Dowmetal is now realized. It is serving industry in an ever broadening capacity and finding its way into the homes of people—to gladden their hearts and lighten their labors.

THE DOW CHEMICAL COMPANY, MIDLAND, MICHIGAN

Branch Sales Offices: 30 Rockefeller Plaza, New York City • Second and Madison Streets, St. Louis • 135 South La Salle Street, Chicago

DOW

CHEMICALS INDISPENSABLE TO INDUSTRY

1950s

Lucky girl indeed! Although any woman this attached to her knives is probably in anger management classes.

Lucky Girl!

she's got *Sky-line* 'CHEF' CUTLERY — it's hollow-ground

'Sky-line' new Chef hollow-ground cutlery is getting a warm welcome from housewives for it's really good looking, utterly practical in the kitchen . . . and is so reasonably priced. Such a variety of knives meet every cutting need, with Sheffield stainless steel blades hollow-ground for lasting sharpness and smart rosewood handles to give you a comfortable grip. Attractively boxed, these modern aids in the home make wonderful gifts too. You can also choose individual knives from the self-service 'Sky-line' display at your dealers.

These are the popular 'Chef' sets by 'Sky-line'

4005 5-piece set as illustrated above (Paring, Utility, French Cook's, Carving and Bread Knives) ... Price 30/-
4032 2-piece carving set (Carving Knife and Fork) ... Price 15/6
4026 3-piece carving set (Carving Knife, Fork and Steel) ... Price 25/-
4043 3-piece boxed set (Carver, Bread and French Cook's Knives) ... Price 21/6
4033 Carded set (Cook's, Utility and Paring Knives) ... Price 10/11

Also obtainable as singles pieces from 2/11 at your favourite store or ironmonger.

Hightime you had Sky-line   *they start sharp—stay sharp*

By the makers of (Prestige) housewares

1950s

And if he catches you using instant coffee, he'll lock you in the basement for a week.

1950

If this is really her idea of a perfect day, then she is on some serious meds.

"Perfect Day!"

Typing all day is easy and effortless when you have an IBM Electric. All you do is "touch" the keys—the typewriter does the work. At five o'clock you'll still feel fresh and free from fatigue.

You'll like all the energy-saving features of the IBM Electric, its simple operation, its perfect impressions, its modern styling. You'll like having the world's finest typewriter for your own.

 IBM *Electric Typewriters*

INTERNATIONAL BUSINESS MACHINES CORPORATION

IBM, Dept. B 3
590 Madison Avenue, New York 22, N. Y.

☐ I'd like to see a demonstration of the IBM Electric Typewriter.

☐ Please send brochure.

Name (please print)

Company

Address

ISN'T GEORGE SWEET . . . Leaving it there for me to find. He knew how I hated our old sink. And now this heavenly surprise. Leisure of all things. Nothing but the best for George. It looks so right and is so sensible. That ultra-deep bowl. Positively masses of draining board. And such a wonderful white. Obviously designed by a woman. But it was bought by my George. Bless him! IN WHITE OR COLOURED VITREOUS ENAMEL FROM £6.6.0 OR STAINLESS STEEL (FITTINGS EXTRA). MADE FOR LEISURE OR OTHER CABINETS.

Allied Ironfounders LEISURE
Leisure Works, Long Eaton, Notts.

NAME _____

ADDRESS _____

_____ HWLS1/11

SHOWROOMS: 141 REGENT STREET, LONDON W1

LEISURE SINKS MADE BY **ALLIED IRONFOUNDERS**

1960s

I'm not sure George is so confident about his gift—looks like he's poised for a quick exit through the window in case she throws it at him.

Acknowledgements

Most images used in this book were provided by the Advertising Archives. The exceptions are those on pp. 20, 22, 23, from *The Art of Looking Good* by Linda Abrams; pp. 34, 36, 42, 72, from the Arents Collection of the New York Public Library; p. 37, kindly supplied by Minnie Fingerhut; p. 46, from the collection of Peter Yarrow and pp. 52, 86, from the Pine Grove Mill collection. Thank you to the companies and products featured for permission to reproduce their advertisements. Particular credits are as follows:

P. 58 reproduced by kind permission of White Castle System, Inc., All Rights Reserved. P. 61 reproduced by kind permission of the National Confectioners Association.

Every effort has been made to trace, contact and credit the copyright holders of the images reproduced. Any further information pertaining to copyright will be included in future editions.

ISBN: 978 193 3176-20-8

Published by Red Rock Press

RED ROCK PRESS

New York New York

info@redrockpress.com

Library of Congress Cataloging-in-Publication Data

Parker, Kate, 1977-
  Outrageous ads : meet your father's automobile, the nervous housewife,
the smoking doctor & the bearded baby! / Kate Parker.
    p. cm.
  ISBN-13: 978-1-933176-20-8
  1. Advertising--United States--History. 2. Commercial products--Social
aspects--United States. 3. Advertising--Pictorial works. I. Title.
  HF5813.U6P34 2008
  659.10973--dc22

                            2007031563

Major portions of this book were first published and copyrighted in 2007 by New Holland Publishers (UK) Ltd
London • Cape Town • Sydney • Auckland

Reproduction by Modern Age Repro House Ltd, Hong Kong
Printed and bound by Craft Print International Pte Ltd, Singapore